THE URBAN GRIOT SPEAKS

by

R. L. Wise

Copyright © 2004 by Ronald L. Wise

All rights reserved. No part of this book my be reproduced or transmitted in any form or by any means, electronic or mechanical, including photocopying, recording or by any information storage and retrieval system, without permission in writing from the publisher.

Published by DaChosen Publishing
Stone Mountain, Georgia
http:/www.dachosen.com/

Cover Design: *Nicole Johnson*
Back Cover Photographer: *Anton Galvin*
In House Editor: *Tracey Wingfield*
Developing Editor: *Quyionah Wingfield*
Typesetter: *Meredith Wingfield*

Printed in the Untied States

Library of Congress Cataloging-in-Publication Data available upon request.

ISBN - soft cover 0-9762627-0-3
ISBN - e-book 0-9762627-8-3

For My Mother

Olga M. Adams-Wise

(1948-2001)

Table of Contents

Table of Contents 1
Black Light 3
Poet to Poet 4
In time 5
THANKS SWEET MAMA WANDA 1 6
Little Thoughts 7
Isolated 8
Difficult Position 9
Fishing for the Dead 10
Freeze! 11
Green Grass 13
THANKS SWEET MAMA WANDA 2 14
Head work 15
Confused 17
Da Hood 18
In Our City Obituary 19
THANKS SWEET MAMA WANDA 3 28
Intellectual Iraq 3/28/04 29
Hopeful 31
Color People Time (Cpt) 32
Day dream 34
All that jazz 35
Brown Sugar Poet 36
C-Low 37
Broken Blues 38
Bending Metal 39
And I See, ... 41
Auction House 43
Untitled (1) 44
Lost Poems 45
Masks of Clay 46
Maybe Next Time 48
Misunderstood 49
Perpetrator 76' 50

Passion	*52*
One Day	*53*
Pay Back	*54*
Straight-Laced 3/23/04	*56*
Picture Wonderland	*57*
Just Thinking of You	*59*
Politics on the Subway at 5	*60*
Position Difficult (remix)	*61*
Predator	*62*
Questions???	*63*
Shoebox poem	*64*
A Poem for Etheridge	*65*
So much on my mind- (Fuck)	*66*
Sounds	*69*
Stoneface	*71*
My streets	*74*
The Aftermath	*76*
The Justice Systems Plan	*77*
The Hold Back	*80*
Thinking Time	*81*
Streets II	*82*
Unmarked Grave	*84*
Tuff Crowd	*86*
Wasn't meant to be	*87*
Tomorrow/ Today (Still Me)	*89*
When She Sings	*91*
The Deal	*92*
Small Town	*93*
Words on the page	*94*
Bloodlines	*96*
Writers block	*97*
To My Wife	*99*
Reflections of a raindrop	*100*
Words to the Blue	*101*
Stranger	*102*
The Chair	*103*

Black Light

Who am I?

I'm black, I'm light

Light,

the skin I'm in,

Like a car driven on the streets,

paint job just right, but yet still I'm light; throughout

life wit my skin- very tight,

Tight like the chains, tight!

Tight like the boats, very tight!

Which held my ancestors, and

consumed their lives.

I'm light, sometimes mistaken for white.

But this-

this light skin I'm in, is very tight, tight like my

black hair, which is not mistaken for white.

But yet I'm still light,

Black,

Black light-

Poet to Poet

Baraka-
Don't leave me hangin,
Lyrics hitt'in hard like I just ran into a gray
like Ms. Johnson's hair
Brickwall-
Full of graffiti
-R. I. P. little Sean-
a sign blows in the wind
"HELP! FeED THE POor"
pour me a drink and make it strong-
Like Baraka's poems
touching deep into my soul

In time

who will I turn to/ when the Heatwave is too much/

can I ride the groove line for free/

while holding those fond memories of you close to my heart/

love is life/ life is love when you and I are one

but who will catch the raindrops when they decide to fall/

visions of me in some type of ghetto dream/

dancing to a song wit a familiar beat/

"I Love Music

Any Kinda Music"

and the O' jay bird sang in my ear/

as a taste of honey touch my lips- she quickly disappeared

THANKS SWEET MAMA WANDA
DREAMS FOR SALE (1)

dark corners
i stand on them
the light
is warm
I am here to fuck-
you up and then
go home

customers frown
light
burns my lips
as the bud
hits the ground

outside
i count my cash
it's been a good night
the street is tight
i head up-   town
i am hungry
i am high

i know what
life is all about

Little Thoughts

Urban Voices get closer

As my choices grow dark

A

Rose grew in Harlem

three blocks

down a child was shot

buck shots

jump shots

an old man's heart just

stopped

chess pieces covered

the ground

Unfortunately all the cars just watched…

Isolated

Great pains of depression
often separate me from the world,
trapped here in my own self-contained
hell-
Lost in the woods, with no flashlight
to guide, so I stumble back and forth
with no concept of time-
Which keeps me literally, looking, lost,
lusting for that complete fix, or sometimes
just sitting mediating here in thee abyss

Difficult Position

My dilemma at hand

clearly puts me in between

the devil and the deep blue sea

But

as I'm trapped here

in this uncomfortable spot

I fight to get out

of my boat

which is lost helplessly at sea…

Fishing for the Dead

I woke up this morning, dipping my hands in a gold bowl
splashing the water on my face praying all alone
job complete from day to day but never done
messages sent to the valleys
of the lost and friends who don't speak
are kept trapped visually in side my dome
Some, maybe a few would understand,
But lives crossed paths
and concert bridges wit dotted lines broken in half
kept us and the world from communicating
but cell phones held us together on wavelengths that
we're over Charged for
and can't break free of
And those friends are still trapped in my dome
waiting to get out
but I keep a hold on them like- lottery tickets
ready to be cashed in
But
the numbers don't match the daily pick so I don't win
And those visions in my head are probably the best friends
I'll ever have
So that's why they'll stay trapped
deep in the riverbed which is embedded in my brain…

Freeze!

Will I be your next victim?

    Just another colored face in the crowd

YES!

Or will you bumrush my ass?

    Fifteen or more just to get me down

NO!

Maybe you'll pull out your guns, and tell me

    "Come on buddy put it down"

PUT WHAT?

    It's just my cellphone!

BOOM!!

But now there's blood all around

DROP!

Can't you see I'm HUMAN, and I pose no

THREAT,

but you pile on top and grab me by my neck.

DAMN!

Let's not forget, that I have a hole in my chest-

    But you proceed to handcuff, and turn me on my side-

Reading me my rights
   as I slowly close my eye's
DAMN!
Will I awake?
   probably not-
But the crowd saw it all-
   Another innocent man-
SHOT!

Green Grass

Blades of grass-

Crushed beneath my feet

Blades of grass

Short, long, brown, and green

Blades of grass-

cool, and soft home to many feet.

Blades of grass

sprinkled, mowed, and

Shit on

by many things in the street.

Blades of grass-

Soft to the touch of my face

But-

not as soft as my ladies legs.

Blades of grass

Everywhere-

even the city has its share.

Blades of grass-

from the beginning of time

Blades of grass-

Till the end of mine....

THANKS SWEET MAMA WANDA
DREAMS FOR SALE (2)

my woman here arm
i hold/ we flood the city
she is strong
under fire
here i am in love

she goes
i stay
she conquers

night falls into
tears/sweet
in my bed
i shake- lips
cracked, eyes role

finally
she stops
we are one
down to the bone

next day will come

Head work

Waiting…

and- waiting…

knowing, that today black bombers

would fire at my broken heart

where choices are

fearful, but hopeful

for today

still knowing

that

Third world countries

hold poison flowers

But

Majority rule wins-

and mirror images of myself

often, wish that they could go

back in time and search the depths

of their character's

while taking long walks

in

the cool summer breeze

Knowing…

and knowing…

Waiting, under the dark moon

where my soul mate would stand

protecting me- from myself

In this world where labels, make you wrong

But I'm

Falling…

Drowning…

Still fearful, but hopeful

camping inside my own words.

This is human- nature's lesson

Sitting…

Resting…

On a granite stone

Confused

                                              Here's a poem-

That might make you

                                              Stop-

     Look-

                 Listen-

Observe, Observe-   Observe------

what's around you

                                       This same poem

might make you

                     Think-

   Blink-

and Wonder, Wonder---

what's going on around you?

                                       This poem

might not do anything-

                                          at all

but stare at you from this page.

                                       Here's a poem

Da Hood

In da hood-

In da hood you hear gun shots in the air at night

    Clap-   Cla Clap, Clap! Clap Clap!

in da hood it ain't nothing like seeing the cops flying

through the streets running all the lights

      In da hood-

in da hood you got young kids mak'in bread

In da hood not everybody gets fed

      In da hood-

in da hood people get profiled, stopped, and arrested on sight

In da hood you might find love for the first time

    In da hood-

in da hood not everyone's looking for a fight

In da hood people have to be up before daylight

        In da hood-

in da hood a rose might grow

But-in da hood you have to

Protect it

To see your little rose with no thorns grow old.

In Our City Obituary
(Imitation of Puerto Rican Obituary by Pedro Pietri)

They didn't work
They were always late
They were never ever on time
They always spoke back
When they were insulted
They didn't work
They always took days off
that were marked as important
-Everyday seemed right-
They were always on strike
from the Man
They worked
but on the block
And were paid
from peoples problems
They worked
They worked
They worked
and they died
They died with chump change in their pockets
They died owing
They died never knowing
what the entrance of the city bank looked like

Jason
Miguel
Tay
Tracy
Manuel
All died yesterday today
and will die again tomorrow

passing their bill collectors
and legal problems
on to the next of kin
All died
waiting for their
cash cow to come in
All died
dreaming about the streets
waking them up in the middle of the night
Screaming: Stop Stop
Please don't shoot
All died
hating the place where
it took place
hating that grocery store
that sold them make-believe
chicken and bullet-proof rice
and beans before they died
All died waiting dreaming and hating

Dead Blacks, and Puerto Ricans
who never cared about Blacks
and Puerto Ricans who always took beer breaks
from the Ten Commandments to KILL KILL KILL
the people of their community
and never communicated with
their lost souls

Jason
Miguel
Tay
Tracy
Manuel
would never breakdown

in the streets
where the rats live like millionaires
and the people do not live at all
are still dead and were never alive

Jason
died right on his stoop
Miguel
died face down with five dollars in his pocket
Tay died on his own supply
Tracy died waiting for a welfare check
That never came
Manuel died waiting for a hit
Addiction
is a long trip
from New York
to upstate cemeteries in between
where they were buried
First the train
and then the bus
and the cold cuts for lunch
and the flowers
that would be stolen
when visiting hours are over
Is very expensive
Is very expensive
But they knew the deal
and their family members
knew it too
Is a long non-profit ride
from New York to upstate
cemeteries

Jason
Miguel
Tay
Tracy
Manuel
All died yesterday today
and will die again tomorrow
Dreaming
Dreaming about the streets
and the Ghetto scene
Million-dollar projects
that collect first of the month checks
keeping Blacks and Hispanics oppressed

These dreams
These empty dreams
from the crack filled streets
to the two bedroom apartments
wit assorted
family members sleeping everywhere
but the television showed
them programs wit how family
was suppose to be
theirs didn't match
except for the black maids
and Latino janitors
who co-existed in their family
circles
Bill collectors laugh at them and their
family which they represent

Jason
died dreaming of that
candy apple red benz

Miguel
died dreaming of that
plasma screen
you know the one I mean
Tracy
died dreaming about
the lottery
Manuel
died dreaming about trying
to quit

They all died
like shrimp dies
in the ritzy restaurants
ashes to ashes
Cocktail sauce to wine
they all died

They knew
they were born to cry
and receive their
felonies under a flag
that lies
the same flag that
misspelled mispronounced
and misunderstood their names
and celebrated when death
came

They were born dead
and they died dead

In a time

when large buildings
are built and then
come down
and visit the number
one healer and fortune
card dealer in town
She can communicate
With those from Nine Eleven
Rest In Peace

Rise Table Rise Table
death is not dumb and disable
those who died, died working
they will show you the way
even though you lived your
life in vain
 Now that your problems are over
and the world is off your shoulders
help those you left behind
find peace of mind
RISE TABLE RISE TABLE

Jason
Miguel
Tay
Tracy
Manuel
All died yesterday today
and will die again tomorrow
Hating fighting and stealing
broken dreams from each other
participating in a trade
that is a trade-off

They are dead
They are dead
and will not return from the dead
until they stop neglecting
themselves and the human race
they will always be dead
never smiling but profiling
always catching a case
the system and drugs
kept and keeps them in
their place
Jason
died hating Miguel because
Miguelmade to much bread in one day
Miguel died hating Tay because
Tay didn't play no games
when it came to getting paid
Tay died hating Tracy because
Tracy had a gun
nickel plated twenty-two
safety off RUN!
Tracy died hating Manuel because
 Manuel always got the good shit
Manuel died hating on them all because
they hated on him for having the most drugs

And now they are together
in the place where
sinners reside
Addicted to silence
off limits to the cool breeze
confined to the worms
that dwell in upstate
cemeteries
this is their hereafter that
waits

Here lies Jason
Here lies Miguel
Here lies Tay
Here lies Tracy
 Here lies Manuel
Who died yesterday today
and will die again tomorrow

Always with chump change
Always owing
Never knowing
that they could change
Never knowing
the geography of their skin
Africa, Puerto Rico are Beautiful places
Africans, Puerto Ricans such Beautiful races

If only they
had turned off the television
and tuned into their history
If only they
had used the knowledge
that was passed on to them
If only they
had thought about genocide
If only they
had kept their eyes open
at the funerals of their
fallen friends
who tried to make a buck
and always had no luck

Jason
Miguel
Tay
Tracy
Manuel
Would right now be doing their own thang
where people of color sing
and dance and work together
where the rain stays away
on summer days
And people of color don't
kill each other but communicate

THANKS SWEET MAMA WANDA
DREAMS FOR SALE (3)

hey woman/you have

a hold on me

grip like a vise

oppressor of the weak

please leave

just go

I need you to stay

your kiss on

my lips tickles

my veins

at least

for now you

cripple my brain

please go

please stay

tomorrow fades

Intellectual Iraq 3/28/04

Statue's toppled, woman cry

Head covered – blackvales crossed the sky

U.S appointed Dictators in power

Many more will rise

bAy of pIgs-

the past rewinds

Bin Ladin slips threw the cracks

Iraqi OIL is the big prize

Prices went uP and now it cost more to drive

Exxon Valdez and soldiers that scream please

children, little boys wit bombs strapped down to their knees

Holy Jihad!

Com'on Bush Please

Triggers that squeeze and Humvees that weave

worst-case scenario is people will bleed

Condoleezza will plead

Colin Powell will lead

Depleted uranium,

Atomic

Nuclear fusion

nine years later adverse heath effects

Senior had the plan and jr. executed it-

Holy Jihad!

Bush you can't win
They won't stop until Allah says end
Battle for Iraq
it's time to rethink it again
I have a dream-
A vision worth more than oil
it burns wit the fury of discontent/to watch many kids die/
so the profit margin can rise
little girls and boys wit tears in their eyes
Who cries for them?
And why?
Al-Qaeda, was wrong but now who's the bad guy
Weapons of mass disappearance
Nothing but lies-
Check the homeland security advisory system-
    IT'S STILL ON HIGH
high as the cocaine that runs through your mind
Friendly fire trapped my thoughts
and chemical warfare burnt my eyes
As pictures are posted the death toll continues to rise…

Hopeful

Take a look inside yourself,

because little things like beauty are only skin deep

If yesterday was a problem- don't worry its now gone

Life is to short

You are who you are,

so its alright to close your eyes and wish upon a star.

because we can't bring back those miserable days-

and who would want to anyway

considering that another bad day is at most just another bad day-

So let it go-

After all if you look inside yourself,

and search the darkness eventually the light you will find.

Another bad day may come- but you will be alright

Alright to smile.

Alright to laugh.

Alright to cry.

and you will be alright to stand on your own when things go wrong

Color People Time (Cpt)

This time it's mine

This time it's mine to hold my head up high,

and search for the faces of friends and kin

This Time it's mine

This Time it's mine to be educated,

and learn the different ways and customs of the past

This Time it's mine

This Time it's mine to hold my spear up high in the air

and-

YELL!

This Time it's mine

This Time it's mine to lower my gun,

and not shoot those same friends and kin but still

YELL!

This Time it's mine

This Time it's mine to grab the shoulders of the people

who held me down

And Shake!

And Shake!

And Shake!

This Time it's mine

This Time it's mine to explore the inner thoughts

of a women in love

This Time it's mine

This Time it's mine to paint my face and pray for those in war This Time it's mine

This Time it's mine to do what ever it is that I wish

So you make your time

because I've made mine

Day dream

Bodies real close

standing face to face-

the curves of your frame make me

not want to wait-

I can-

smell your scent

it's driving me wild, your hairs very beautiful

with a twinkle in your eye-

your lips look soft,

and I wish for one

kiss-

but, not knowing your name makes me continue to wish

All that jazz

        Drop

    Drip   Drip

    Drop Drip

        Drop

The beat of the rhythm doesn't stop

        Drop

    Drip   Drip

    Drop Drip

    Drop Drip

        Drop

Keep it coming is there more in stock?

        Drop

    Drip   Drip

    Drop Drip

    Drop Drip

        Drop

Is it only the sound of my faucet? Or

Can you hear Harlem jazz roar?

        Drop

    Drip   Drip

    Drop Drip

    Drop Drip

    Drop Drip

        Drop

I love it, give me more-

Brown Sugar Poet

Brown sugar poet
Wit your thick full lips
that spit flames
sparks of knowledge
come straight from your brain

-I love that -
Brown sugar poet
Long legacy of pain
your heart pumps blood
but poetry's in your veins
You are a Queen!
don't ever forget
that
you can speak your mind
where ever you're at
cause
"Poet to Poet"
I'll forever have your back

C-Low

Dice game,

Faces change,

bullets are exchanged

Money flies

you go hide

and now it's not a game

Snake eyes,

was rolled

you go cold-

But still the game is played

Broken Blues

Albany, New York blues

and muddy waters- A Mississippi moans

Sing it Bessie!

But the dark was the

night

and cold was the ground

I had love in my veins-

But was it the

stormy Monday blues

that made

Bobby Bland?

T'aint nobody's bizness

Have you heard?

I still got love in my veins-

But now the thrill is gone

Bending Metal

Hold my hand tight,
as we cross underneath the night sky
like cabs racing for their next job-
Horns, honking and lights as bright as the night stars-
keep my hand vise tight, so my world won't collapse
here under the pressure of others is where we relax
      Did you see those lights?
Taken to the depths of our, wine riddled bodies
emotions spark, but I should have been a fire cracker,
lost in the pack never to see the fourth of July-
But those damn lights from those cabs
keep blinding my eyes
      Did you see those lights?
Oh how I wish I could steal a kiss
but the appliance for misalignment
is blocking loves blitz-
      Look there go those lights again!
Those lights-
like the one's when I was young,
hanging above the streets
illuminating everything below

Those lights-

beating down stony brick paths

with no way to the future

and no way to the past

      Look there go those lights!

And I See,

And I See,

I See shades of movement from objects unknown.

And I See,

I See the faces of my family for the first time;

And I See,

I see myself starting to crawl, walk, run and play.

And I See,

I see discipline,

in the form of my father's belt for the first time.

And I See,

I see Christmas, Thanksgiving,

and New Years go one by one.

And I See,

I see the physical abuse of my father towards my mother.

And Then I See,

My father getting "the hell out" like my mother told him.

And I See,

I see myself growing tall.

And I See,

I see myself being attracted to girls.

And I See,

I see the opposite sex necked for the first time.

(Yeah!)

I See, touch, and feel

And I See,

I see adulthood coming on.

And I See,

I see death of a young black male who was slain

(better, make it 1,2,3,4,5,6,7)

well you understand what I'm trying to say.

And I See,

I see the beauty in both my daughters' eyes.

And I See,

I see my mother gone, resting for eternal time.

And I See,

I see myself growing old, holding my first grandchild.

And I See,

I see my mother, grandmother, grandfather,

and different figures of people from my past

greeting me.

Oh Yeah! I See…

Auction House

"Female, Negro for sale!"

Probably raped on the ship.

"Two for one deal!

male Negro with a kid;"

Grandfather, and Grandmother, sold at half price.

This is what took place

in the Auction house year round, day and night.

As I stare and look around,

I wonder how long it took to build

with all the wood, windows, and doors intact.

Was that day cold or was it hot?

Did the rain beat down on the heads of the oppressors?

Or, was it built by the slaves; who soon would be sold?

These are the questions I ask myself to write about so this I must,

China glass and Queensware Auction house all full of dust,

Slaves, in the back corralled like cows.

Slaves, in the front lined shackled and bound.

Fingers are pointed; little black kids are kicked.

I often wonder how many times, they were struck by a whip.

Untitled (1)

As I stand on this boardwalk

gazing at the ocean for miles

and miles

The water slaps the docks

like my father slapped my mom

Lost Poems

Flashbacks in time
showed me the truth
Dreams-
seasons lost in the dark
pieces of my memories
those poems that I forgot
and
my pen which dripped blood
instead of ink
causing a pack of starving wolves
to come and put me out of my misery
Those wolves
wit their red eyes and pointed teeth
made me reach the end of my line
crossed in the sand and filled with regret
those words I couldn't
remember the lost poems which
depended on me to spit
but the best I could come up wit
is "get back wolves cause I don't take no shit"
To my surprise they did
get back
and now I stand here alone
in fear that those poems will never ever return

Masks of Clay

Clay masks shaped and molded the
face-
Life on the streets is such a waste
So they say-
Clean out your locker
and throw your things away
base hits might get cha there, but home runs
win games
touchdowns, three pointers
it's all the same

Clay mask crack wit heartache and pain

And I'm often confused when asked
What is your race?
What is my race!
Exactly what is yours?
And when is the last time you placed?

but you see I'm not quick,
although my mind likes to run
I often wait for
June-
cause that's when the new
Jordan's- come

But those clay masks keep watching me
shaking their heads in
Shame

life's not a joke
so stop pretending it's a
Game
on the streets lives change

you could be arrested like
Paul Raul for something you say-
Or you could fall short like the
Stock Exchange,
Mixed cash and greed controls the day

How long will that last?
Those clay mask finally ask-

Maybe Next Time

Not to far away our eyes

meet-

short feet

deep breath in between-

A glance to the right, one slightly left

Can I have your number?

Now it's finally off my

Chest-

looking down, and up

then a stare through my soul

slow words come out your mouth

N-O-

Misunderstood

Flakes of paint-

red, yellow, purple, and blue

As

lights fade out

What's a child to do?

Hands touching to feet

Wit-

ankles in between

lighting strikes on my chastised bare yellow ass

and I ask again-

What's a child to do?

Perpetrator 76'

he lowered

her panties down

dripping

wit the smell of virgin oil

bathroom talk is cheap

but the wolf panting

knew how to cum.

perched/watching

quick hands

"isn't she lovee- ly

isn't she wondeerful"

hand on her ass

pLeAsE

cOm'oN

still perched

pubic hair

just barely

in

fingers the size of

hot-dog links

fried in a pan winking,

grinning

shit eaten smile

sweat roll'in

down backs

screams, music

eye's wide lOOking

"isn't-she-love-ly

made-from-love"

cries from her eye's

too mine

remembering that smile

Passion

The red wine

tickled the back of her throat

While a hint of

Spring

blew softly by the

tip of her nose

Barry White played low in the

background

and love was in the air-

But it was she who sat

complacent and alone…

One Day

Hours tick, the sunshine, shines

cigarette butts are flicked

radio blasting, playing jiggas the city is mine.

Car doors are kicked; people don't give a fuck

city streets are polluted with garbage, and drugs

Me, I just chill

and try to do my thing

Surviving in a world where fear is king.

Pay Back

My pay back won't consist of no

Guns-

Knives-

Bats-

or bricks-

to get my point across

Oh no! this pay back may leave you

dazed-

confused-

and lost in the sauce

My pay back-

My pay back won't be televised

but when it starts I'm sure you'll be

green wit envy, and all choked up inside.

The pay back will be bittersweet,

that they'll package it up and sell it on e-bay for a week

My pay back-

My pay back might make you see things

Clear-

or it might just be something you can't

get out of your ear-

pay back-

pay back will be something you're not even looking for

so if you test me, pay back will be inevitable

Straight-Laced 3/23/04

That white picked fence, for instance
in the front yard of the vacant house:
Men winked and whistled at
the long legs, full lips
it would take days to
understand the pain
she showed on her face

Her body's no longer pure, but her thoughts are free
She can stroll at will, day
light yellow then black
as the bottom of an oversized
tire on a run down pickup

but as she took her steps
The picked fence, fell down like cinderblocks,
those whistles and winks kept her alive-
she would never stop…

Picture Wonderland

Eight different pictures
on the wall of mothers home-

sun drawn, chains broken
African King with his chest out

Little old woman,
hat tilted to the side
pain on her face, stillness
of pride

Eight different pictures
on the wall of her home-

River of trust,
with a crowd on it banks
preachers hands on the back,
of one disciples neck

Four little boys,
faces ready and game
one wit a stick,
must have been caught in mid-play

Eight different pictures
on the wall of her home-

Egyptian princess,
skin beautiful
chin held high, and proud

Picture of a flower,
the largest on her wall
blossomed to perfection

wit a frame made of gold

Eight different pictures
on the wall of her home-

Little black girl,
dressed in pink,
hands on the black and white keys
ready to sing

Two pictures down,
is a portrayed of me

Just Thinking of You

Dear Mommy,

It seemed like yesterday when things were ruff in our house,

just you, Josette, Michael, and I with all the lights out.

Times were tough, but some how you pulled ahead,

Ma;

I can't seem to forget Stevie Wonder

playing in the background

and me jumping on my bed.

I realize now the discipline you had to instill;

because it's rough being a black woman

and trying to raise us to be men.

I miss you so much and I wish you could be here,

but the lord had something else in mind

when he took you to be there.

I was looking at your photo just the other day

when I thought I heard your voice,

it seemed like so far away,

but I'm sure you were near me cause my tears wiped away.

As I got up to stand, I felt your fingers go in my hair,

then your voice said to me.

"Son I'll always be here."

To my mother Olga M. Wise (1948-2001)

Politics on the Subway at 5

Papers wit news of yesterday's race
who understood cross talk
why are these old white men in suites telling me my place
some crooked face man stared off into space
posters warped by
causing my head to ache
yellow platform lines kept running for days
endlessly in my mind the sound would stay
trains on the other tracks screamed in pain
men on this particular train seemed ready to throw their
hats into the political race hoping for change.

But no one cares what they think.
loud and out of control
Four politically incorrect kids
started to explode
as our train screeched to a halt
three of the four misunderstood got off
loud voices behind me sounded like horns
one little old woman held her pocketbook
close to her soul

And the train kept pushing on
Orange and brown seats
kept us in our place
while those same men
continued their talk about our
Presidential state.

Position Difficult (remix)

Helplessly at sea

my boat

which I fight to get out of

but

is lost

clearly I'm trapped

in this uncomfortable spot

as my dilemma at hand

puts me in between the devil and

the deep blue sea…

Predator

Lying on top of the grass- with the hot, sweltering sun on my back.
Watching my prey while I roll over to relax.
I wait for a second then let out a yawn.
Now they see me the king of them all.

Questions???

Tripped on a curb
Little jonnie
fell victim to the world
wit all its
Disrespect,
Narrow-minded,
Prejudice people, who plague it.
Who the hell is he to change things/
maybe one day his daughter
might ask
Why-
Why do they say I'm not
Black?
Why-
Why do they say I'm not
White?
and jonnie in his deep voice
might say
You- are you
don't worry just lead
And wit no thought at all picked himself up
but the curb was still hard…

Shoebox poem
(To the old man in Grand Central Station)

Shoe box

box the shoe

the box is the shoe-

Or maybe shoe is the box

but don't forget to grab

the

Shoebox…

A Poem for Etheridge

Brother Knight I read your poems and studied them well.
Just like your 47 pictures, on the wall of your cell.

I've thought long and hard about robbery and crime, cause you
see I too was incarcerated not for eight years; but a small
Stretch of time.
And although my time was short, I believe we thought the same,
that the system in it's self is a sense of slavery all over again.
So now I work hard, hard as a rock but not to remember my
name.
Because unlike *hard rock*
I haven't returned from the hospital for the criminally insane.
But you see *television speaks*
And *A fable* is told
black males are confused, I definitely think not.
So this is my mission to keep on writing to do my part;
and keep the system from capturing another young black heart.
Brother Knight, *I'm not a black poet, who thinks of suicide,*
but I wish, I wish you could go back and redo 1985.
Peace Brother Knight!

So much on my mind- (Fuck)

Time for getting fucked has always been around…

But I ain't down with all the fucking

that goes on around the world and in this town.

    Crackdealers-

Fucking their own kind.

Fucked up!

    So the over paid crooked cops

fuck the dealers by giving them Consecutive time.

    Justice system, Rockefeller drug laws

Fuck!

I mean were getting fucked everyday

    Health insurance is up.

So were Fucked!

    Heat and electric companies have a monopoly

Guess what Fucked Again!

    Gas prices went up

We got Fucked!

    Hell-

the movie prices went from twenty-five cents,

to three dollars and fifty cents,

to nine dollars

I would consider that getting Fucked!
        Seeing as though half the movies made sucked.
Awhile back you could get a new car for three grand,
   now you can't even get an American made car for less
than twenty grand
    That's Fucked!
You know what's fucked, fucked is your Tell-Lie-Vision,
which shows skinny people
eating burgers and fries wit diet sodas
That's fucked up!
 Radio stations playing the same songs
over,
and over,
and over again
That's fucked! Change the format- Please!
Politics-
How about those politicians?
Where are all the bombs in Iraq?
Fuck!
        North Korea has them all…
Now that's fucked!
Tax dollars for George W's plan-
       We all just got fucked into World War three!
I'm tired of getting fucked

So here are some other people who also got fucked
" but Worst then me"
Nelson-
      Martin
Malcolm
    Marvin
Medgar-
   Yusuf
Emmett-
      Huey
All Fucked!
Since they were fucked
here's some people and things I'd fuck
Cable TV-
    It cost too much
The tabacco industry
         Stop polluting my air
The governor of New York-
      Hell! just get him the fuck out
And George W.
     What's it all about?
Oil!
Hell we all just officially been fucked!

Sounds

Train whistles roar-
Airplanes soar-
gray concrete blocks surround
the neighborhoods door to door

Cops soar-
Fire engines roar-
sidewalks leak blood
wit burnt down buildings next to liquor stores

Leafs blow, trees grow, rain, snow
And New York's traffic -flows-
times and places change
plus all the things I've been wanting to say

I sat in my room for hours listening to Coltrane
my mind was Miles away
as the gin flowed through my blood stream
and Coltrane seemed to play
the same notes over and over just for me

A Byrd landed on my ledge as I swallowed the liquid sin
Cats in the alley never stayed quite
even at night when the trumpets blew wind

Fire engines roar-
Airplanes soar-
Dizzy I got as I fell to the floor
Louis's arm was strong as he pulled me up

the honey in the corner of the room never shut up
and bebop, plus cool jazz, was a part of the scene
I lifted my glass when Holiday sang
Showing praise to the queen…

Stoneface

Stoneface was a cat
we all knew from back when-
back when-
We all played in the sandlot
that's where his name began
hit in the face
that rock changed him for real
cause you see
Stoneface never played in the lot again

Stoneface was a cat
we all knew from back when
back when-
Stevie sang about ribbons in the sky
that was the Stoneface we all knew back then
he wore blue converse and never ever grinned
that scar changed him and his circle of friends
Yeah!
We all knew Stoneface
way back when
Back when-
Breakdancin was in

Damn!
Stone could really backspin
Back when
Back when-
Shelltoe and fatlaces was in
Stoneface was cool back then-

Stoneface was a cat
we all knew from back when
back when-
Public Enemy fought the power
and
Black Consciousness was in
raiders coats wit the hats to match
Stoneface was Chuck D.
and just like that, that was that
cause you see drugs came on the scene
and that's when he earned his name for real
crack gobbled him up and he became a kingpin

Stoneface was a cat

we all knew from back when

Back when-

The cops kicked in his door and killed

his little kid

Damn!

Stoneface was never the same

I saw him a few days after he did his long jail stay

in an alley shooting heroin in his veins

Stoneface was a cat

we all knew from back when

Back when-

Those same drugs brought him to his end

Stoneface was a cat

We all knew form back when

Back when Back when…

My streets

Time is ticking, and the streets are watching.
A gunshot is heard a life was just taken.
I walk down the street just a little bit further,
A crackhead is laid out
on the concrete stoop while kids wander by,
Crack vile's are kicked,
And a mother let out a yell
"Anton! Get your ass in this house."
Then there was aloud slap,
but it wasn't Anton, who was standing far to my left.
It was the tall dark brother on the corner
who had just been checked.
His girl small in stature had caught him with a left
an old man on his steps turned and let off a grin.
Oh damn! I just stepped in dog shit again.
I run into the corner store with my head held high,
but before I enter I take a look around.

Maybe I'll trade it

these crazy streets of mine,

or maybe I'll stay until it's my time.

But these-

These streets filled with bums and dirt all around

These are my streets, my city, my town.

The Aftermath

I'm unmotivated
and another day has passed
watching these poets
say painful haiku's
that I don't understand
So I look beyond the devils pawn
and hope
that I come up with something
Strong, or at least a Strong feeling
something kept isolated in my soul
So again I wait to reach my limit
plus I had a conversation with death
because when I'm in my inner space
I never hold back-
Giving birth to masterpieces
Some in their own special way
Rainy days and Sundays
always seem the same
with clusters of poems clogging
up my brain

The Justice Systems Plan
(For Mike and Randy)

Give me three meals

a cot

and a cell

I have to keep clean

LOCK ME UP!

AND THROW AWAY THE KEY!

The justice system has a plan…

I'm Twenty-Something and

Black

The jury of my peers is Sixty- Something

and not to mention all

White

I guess peer pressures a bitch

when your found Guilty!

on all counts

The justice system has a plan…

The Plan-

It's simple

Make sure your labeled

when you're young

This would be strike one!

In the plan your records will be on file

Juvenile status-
It doesn't apply
Strike two!
Is on you, this is made clear
when you see those finger prints from earlier years
Third Strike!
and most important
they just wait for you to slip
loss you're cool-
act the fool-
basic type of shit
The system has a plan…
If you don't believe me
look at the scales
she's not blind folded for nothing
and the E.s.q. knows the real
Ask your court appointed lawyer
he'll copout you a deal
plea bargain down to this
and you won't even need bail
So how about a 6 to 5?
Your young, and a strong black male
Or you can try to press your luck at trial
But if you lose your outta here

They don't care,

and always remember your time tips the scales

The system has a plan…

The system has a plan…

The Hold Back

I'm stuck

in the mud

with these hands

grabbing for control

And spears in my back

ripping through my

flesh and severing my spinal cord

Thinking Time
(For Curtis)

Life's a disaster, trapped here under the masses of-
noncritical thought, neighborhoods with no support,
gun owners with no brains, abortion activists fifty to sixty
year old men- no shame
    -Keep your head together and try not to explode-
Metal dragons still move from North to South, sometimes
they bump heads-
But that's alright!
Stars and moons collapse, movies are made, look at the big
picture to see right where your at
    Stop!
The largest buildings in New York come down,
ashes to ashes dust to dust, "Lets Roll" as the war pushes on
    -Keep your head together and try not to explode-

Streets II

Concrete sidewalks,
bus stops leak blood-

kids and mothers hug,
hug the pipe June bug
keep it close to your soul-

Joel the three legged dog
may not live long

Train tracks run
up and down my mothers arm
Arm yourself it's time to get it on

Revolution!

Fight the power!
The power to fight-
Public Enemy broke up
Now that ain't right

Radios sing,
it's all Bling-Bling
Shame - shame if you snitch
on somebody in the game'

But if you keep snitchin
It's your life the streets will claim

So alley cats wander
in search of food
only to be run down,
and ripped in two-

And you,
you keep lookin
wit that look in your eye
Wondering
Is it my time?
or
Will I survive?

Unmarked Grave

Bullets whistle,
whispers over the dirt,
flowers laid-

Police tape yellow
twisted across the
neighborhood makeshift grave-

Stop sign deserted,
wit your mother's heartache and
pain

Candles lit,
and strategically placed-
leather was your choice
on that faithful day

Soil on your casket
wit no headstone in place
so they gather at your final spot,
exactly one year to the day

But now the flowers have wilted,

many washed away

except for your mother's pain, even harder on this day

And although you are gone,

a single candle

still stays lit

to resemble your heart,

bullets-

shredded it quick

so now we pray,
here under the stop sign
at your unmarked grave-

Tuff Crowd

Down breezy cold concrete streets

the people and their shoes

trampled papers from yesterday's news

While a blind man Sang

and the horns on the cars,

which always blew

sounded like amplified Boo's-

Plus the old blind man was missing out

on the young ladies dress that blew high in the sky

like the pigeons that flew above him

He probably would sing a different tune

and the shoes would sound more like applause

drowning out those cars,

which always seemed to continue to boo

setting him up for the next days news

Cool old blind man sings the blues

and a coin hits his jar breaking the sound of the boo's

Wasn't meant to be

The distance between them provided tension
like cables on a bridge ready to pop and give
Because the hurricane winds made the bridge sway
over the rivers mirror image-

But they kept their cool and did not panic at all
looking for love but their feet were stuck.
Trapped in the mud.
He took another look, and gave her a smile
while the crowd danced to a familiar tune.

She smiled back, but did not follow through-
He waited a second and then decided to take
a chance
It was to late.
As she extended her hand another came from the
crowd
and it was not a man.
they came close and kissed,
then they laughed

Releasing the tension and making him hot
He downed the last of his drink with emotion that could not be stopped.
as he gathered his keys a hand touched him softly on his back
Scared to turn around he stood his ground
for a second and then walked out…

Tomorrow/ Today (Still Me)

I've swam in the depths of the sea,
touched the mountain tops, walked
on grasses that were green, and blown
into the air trees that were mean-
      But I'm still me
Often I've crept through the streets late
at night, spit language and gestures at
people that weren't nice-
kissed my mother before her demise,
tears fell down raining from the sky-
      But
I'm still me
Many times I've run from the cops
when it's time to run,
squeezed triggers on pearl handled guns,
talked a lot of shit, and looked the devil
in his face for fun-
But I'm still me
I've traveled long distances in cars with
no gas, watched the world through double
pane glass, licked my lips,
and drank bottles of champagne-

But I'm still me
I keep my head held high with dreams of
success, sometimes pushed down wondering-
What's next?
often finding time to ask the lord to bless
But I'm still me

When She Sings

When she sings

her smooth tender voice melts my eardrums-

she always hits

every note high and low.

When she sings

she stays right on key,

and the baseline is low-

She is the Queen of R&B.

She is the sister of the soul.

The Deal

Lost in the confusion
   of the streets
black hooded sweatshirt
   wit the-
chrome piece underneath
designer boots, jeans
   and a
fistful of green-
   You know me,
the local neighborhood American dream-
So what the deal?
White dust mixed, and baked into little powered
   balls-
if your lucky you can get two for fifteen and start the
   rush flow-
Go ahead and go berserk sell what ever you can-
   but-
from me to you
   no hard feelings
it's just supply and demand

Small Town
(Outside the Three Story Building Window in Schenectady, N.Y)

There's a lot going on in this small town-

to many things that I don't understand

Big-to-small things,

some good/some bad

There's always something going on in this small town-

Life-

    Death-

it goes on.

Just like your town-

But!

this town is small…

Words on the page

The words you see on this
page
are my thoughts
A gift-
Sometimes good and evil…
born from the spirits of yesterdays poets
Like-
G. Moses Horton,
Claude Mckay,
Zora Neale Hurston,
James Weldon Johnson,
Paul Dunbar,
Etheridge Knight,
Gwendolyn Brooks,
and Langston Hughes…

The givers,
who made you believe in their words
Do I have that ability?
Yes, No, Maybe so!
or will I regret what I write?
No!

Ask Amiri Baraka-
He'll probably tell me to "keep pushing on"
and when I "push"
Sometimes it might be darkness
that spills onto these pages
But-
If you keep searching, you'll find the light
in between those
use to be blank spaces

Now I'm not alone nor am I the chosen one
because we all have been selected
with some gift of spoken word
But-
this here is just a note to you poets who forgot-
The poetry clubs in session
whether you like it or not…

Bloodlines
(For Huey, and Fred)

As the sun faded and the streetlights clicked

Gun smoke broke the sky taking his breath with it

The blood which once flowed wit life now circled in a pool

Drifted treasures taken to soon

Writers block

I need to write
so I open up this book

To make it all right
lyrically you might think it's nice
this book with these words and phrases in it
but as you read this book
there is a question, which is asked

Will I continue to write?

Or will I take long trips
and forget how to write-
Will I on those long trips maybe to the
Bahamas or Puerto Rico
Stick my feet in the white sand
Sipping on ice-tea hand in my pocket
and one placed firmly on the glass-
reflecting on the streets and where I've been

But I continue to write
Pen shaking with affection,
about what I might write
and how it should be done

So I write in this book
sometimes for fun
Will I continue to write?

Ask Jil if she did-
continue to write
or was it something she kept
Bottled up inside

Her answer would be quick
and precise

"What is it that you're trying exactly
not to write?"

So I write…

To My Wife

I remember that night of passion filled with love, sex,
                                                touching, feeling,
                                                and then holding. It
                                                was great!
                                          But now, it's six
months later and your stomach has stretched, our baby is growing inside of you. And I love caressing your beautiful skin, holding you tight, and rubbing your belly sometimes all night. God! I can't wait!
               Is it a boy? Or
                 is it a girl?
                 Are the
                 questions
             we are asked,
           but between you
         and I, we really don't
       care-
    Because what ever we receive,
  our child will truly be blessed, with
the love of both worlds. Now lay back,
I'll rub your feet and you can just rest....

Reflections of a raindrop

Rain falls heavily on the cars

that pass by without a clue

tires turn as the gutter overflows

while I think of you.

Sun breaks through the clouds

as a ray of light touches

the concrete under my feet

and a sweet sensation seems to make

all of life for me complete.

Words to the Blue

Stop!

Stop look'n at me, as I slide by in my ride

Don't!

Don't question me, when I walk- walk on by

Leave!

Leave me alone, when I'm in a group more than two

I have-

I have committed no crime, and did nothing to you

So!

So stay off my case, and give me my space

And maybe-

And maybe we can exist, in the same place.

Stranger

When you see me walking down the street,

don't be afraid to stop and talk to me.

You'll never know what's in this heart of mine

and you won't be disappointed if you'll just take the time.

You'd never walk on by if you could tell,

that no matter who you are I would treat you right.

It actually doesn't matter how you look,

because you never know the content until you open the book.

The Chair

The wood on the deck
flaked endlessly near
My foot-
draped in cloth and water
Filled my
Ear-
Drum in the background
played a beat from the past
the birds started singing
hell the weekend went by
Fast-
Was this girl that I knew from
junior high, I can't remember
her name so I sing a
Lullaby-
To my kids who are sitting
on my lap
Ready to leave in another car
Which-
Is parked right out
Back-
to reality my mind shifts into
 gear –
these are the relaxing days
sitting here in this chair

Special Thanks: AKA - The Shout Outs

There are so many people that I would like to thank who have influenced me in one way or another. Some of you are more influential than others, but in the long run each of you that I have come into contact with has dropped some type of knowledge on me. And for this I'm eternally grateful. First, I must thank my mother Olga (Tracy) M. Wise for blessing me with this gift that she was also blessed with from God. Second, is my family Grace (Gagi) Adams. RIP.1992 (I miss you, and only wish I was old enough mentally to hold an in-depth conversation with you), Inez (Nana) Wise-Johnson (I'm thankful that we have a relationship now, and I only wish we spent more time together when I was younger), My wife Nicole H. Wise (You have been the sole person who has pushed me in my quest for more knowledge and I love you for that. I could not have asked for a better woman in my corner), Arianna O. Wise, Chloe M. Wise (My two Beautiful girls "Daddy loves you." My brothers and sisters- Michael G. Parris, Josette M. Wise, Joseph "Baby Boy" Wise Jr., Durand Bennett- Wise, Fatima Thompson-Wise, Taquisha Wise,

Joshua Wise I Love you all. My Nieces and Nephews Crystal N. Galvin, Robert J. Galvin III, Anton A. Galvin, Amaris M. Parris, The Adams Family, The Wise Family (James "Uncle Jim" Wise, Geraldine Patterson-Wise, Marcella Simmons-Wise, Clifford Wise, Rosie Thomas-Wise, Clara "Dusty" Hampton-Wise, Leslie "Pibit" Wise, John Wise, Anthony "Uncle Tony" Wise Sr., Sinda "Aunt Sinda" Johnson, Connie and Jenny, Barron Wise and Jeff, and the rest of the Glassboro, N.J family, The Sponable Family (Edward, and Nancy "Thank you for the support over the years, also no more powder blue suits", Chris, Craig, and Jason), The Ballou Family (Elizabeth, Eric, Gregory, Maudtresse, Monique (Thank you for staying close) My brothers by another mother, Timothy "Dj. Timmy Tim" Knight- Good look'in on all the advice, I will never forget any of it. Curtis M. Welcome, Michael L. Fulton, Randy L. Hunt, Kenneth Smith AKA. (Kay, Tightman, Kaydog, Smalldog, Yellowman, etc.), All of you mean the world to me and I could not ask for better BFAM's, you are all truly great in your own unique way. The Welcome Family (Shirley A. Welcome "Mom", Sears "Duke" Welcome Jr., Yolanda J. Welcome, Sylvester "William" Huggins, Chris Huggins) The Fulton Family (Omari "O" Fulton, Joshua Fulton, Jason Fulton (Keep your head up), Hank "Hank! Hank!" Fulton, Mary-Ann Fulton, Tony "Big Tone" Fulton), and the rest of the clan. The Riddick Family (Erica, and Hassan), Faith and Ray James, The Guyer Family, The Smith Family (Greg, Joe, and Bee), Katisha "3rd Ave Poet" Burt "We did it Albany", Nicole Johnson (My Illustrator), Nicole Knight, Ronald "Big John" Motts, Robert "LaMique" Gatlin, George Avramidis, John "3-point Shot" Knapp, Richard Jackson, Lamar and Alex Erwin, Robert Dobbs, Robert "Buff" Thomas, Dj Thomas, Abe Avramidis, Nate "Nate dawg" Stevens, Ann-Marie "Re" Hilts, Crystal Buchanan, Shana Stage, George Rose, Greg Davenport, Chandra Goodwin and the Whole Belmont Popwarner Family, Mr. Marc's Barbershop "Mr. Marc Thompson", Beatrice Wells, 96.3 Sugar Bear, Dj. Royal Crush, Michael A. "Merlin" Davis, Tamu Hassan-Chambers, Dr. Mark Anthony Neal, Dr. Leonard A. Slade Jr., Dr. Sharon Parkinson, Dr. Allen Ballard, Dr. O. Williams, Dr. Maurice Thornton, Dr. Marcia Sutherland, Dr. K. Sarfoh, Dr. Joseph Bowman, Dr. G. Levesque, Professor Joseph Cardillo, Professor Urban-Mead, Dr. Jil Hanifan, SUNY at Albany, Jason "Flowmaster" Seale, Phyllisa Smith, Tracey Wingfield, Kim Wallace, DaChosen Publishing and The Urban National Poets League.

To all others that I could not recall Thank You.

Peace,
Ronald L. Wise

For those who are no longer Physically with us,
but are in Spiritual Essence:
R.I.P-
My Mother Olga M. Wise, Dennis Wise, Michael L. Fulton Sr., Sylvester William "Butch" Huggins Sr., Ike Miller, Shirley Smith, Mark Barry, Shabazz "Big Baz" Fulton, Thaddeus McCray Sr., Nerraw Black, Anita Vrooman, Steph, Ruthie, and Gary Springstein-

www.ingramcontent.com/pod-product-compliance
Lightning Source LLC
Chambersburg PA
CBHW031257290426
44109CB00012B/622